OUR TRUE MISPERCEPTIONS!

Dealing with perceptions……………..

Dr Mona Aeysha Khalid

TABLE OF CONTENTS

DEDICATION

To my Mom and Son, Yahya.

INTRODUCTION:

In this book, you will find something new with regard to perceptions, and their counterpart-misperceptions. Although we all face various kinds of psychological setbacks from time to time, yet a few of us are willing to bring a change. If you are among those, then this book will explore new horizons for you. It will not solve your problems, but guide you how to prevent coming dangers in a better way. This will enrich your understanding of human perceptions and misperceptions so that you could judge yourself and others in the light of true perceptual knowledge. Your misperceptions were going to take you to a blind valley of disappointment, mistrust and guilt but your new perceptions of life will change the root in your brain. Then eventually you will realize that many aspects of life are only due to our misperceptions and nothing else. You will not waste your energy, time and money on unreal, fake and dual personalities. You will distinguish better between genuine and duplicate gestures. You will predict the future better, pass present more creatively and plan for the future wisely. You will be able to save yourself from potential damages, sudden strokes, and being stuck in the way due to unforeseen and unpredictable behavior of your friends, co-workers, and partners.

Hope you will also enjoy the ride and get back to me in the most favorable way.

Mona Aeysha

OUR PERCEPTUAL BACKGROUNDS

To solve our problems we need to find out our pure original disk of concepts in black and white. Indeed, it is very much complicated science. By the time we are not aware of our hidden rooted shaped conceptual backgrounds, we cannot find a clear path to follow to get rid of our misperceptions.

In the scientific study of perceptual psychology, pictures are always painted through their backgrounds. Our color perception is changed by the color/pattern of background only. It will not be wrong to say that there are as many pictures in this world as many backgrounds. Without any background, no picture can exist. Similarly, we behave in our daily life under the influence of certain backgrounds. Sometimes we don't even know what the background effect on our life is.

Background can be anything from any abstract concept to any physical object hidden in our unconscious. For example, a concept can be any trivial statement like, 'I am a woman who needs attention from others or 'I am a mother who is always loving and caring' or 'I am an honest being' or 'I am brave and outspoken', etc. All kinds of confessions and self re-assuring statements are sometimes our hidden backgrounds; of that, even we are not aware. Likewise, feelings

7

(secure/sick/happy/cool/low) associated with events (such as a new-year day, a birthday, a holiday trip) are taken as examples of conceptual backgrounds. Whereas a hill- station, a hotel, a picnic spot, and a tourist attraction can be taken as examples of hard/physical backgrounds. Whenever our background environment (conceptual or physical) changes, our behavior follows and we react in a new manner. Moreover, anything or any concept can become a part of a background consciously or unconsciously by us in a specific moment/event. For example, we miss our home often, whenever we are abroad and miss abroad often whenever we are back at home. In such cases, our both conceptual and physical environments change.

Things that play their role as a background shape our perceptions that are very important for our attitudes. When we are missing someone, we are at the same time ignoring someone else whom we will miss at any other time with different background. Taking another example, suppose you are told about a guy who is having a grand car, big career, fancy clothes, a charming face with a luxurious lifestyle; you will in no time make a good image of him. Then the same time someone tells you that it is all fake- he is a very poor guy indeed and asking for some charity instead. You will again reshape his image and think a little differently at the same time. Here the only background (conceptual) is changed not the guy. You have already seen background effects while making your web sites, editing pictures, watching movies and even selecting outfits with designs.

Have you ever encountered that your boyfriend is behaving differently with you in front of 'a' or 'b'? Have you ever noticed that your son is indifferent to you while sitting in the company of other relatives/friends? Have you ever noticed someone you know from your heart, is behaving odd in his office or at other particular place? Have you ever argued with someone for stating two different contradictory statements at two different places? Have you ever thought people change their attitude due to their diplomatic mind-set? One surly encounters such experiences at least once in his or her lifetime.

However, not all experiences are due to our misperceptions. Some of them are true examples of cheating, diplomacy, and duality. My point, in this regard is that our backgrounds have a strong effect on our thoughts, actions, and attitudes and that (effect) is beyond our expectations. For example, one can become a very positive individual in his parents' company and much negative in his friends' company consciously and unconsciously. One can behave aggressively with his family and at the same time act like a gentleman in his office with co-workers. One can be genius in front of his relatives, and proves criminal for his enemies. There could be a thousand other examples to quote in this regard.

In fact, our backgrounds are our predecessors and predict our behavior strongly. The main backgrounds include: place of experience, thoughts within unconscious, beliefs about the information perceived and any kind of future association.

The place of experience includes all related information about the place at which you are. For example, if you feel secure in your parents' home and love to be there, you will act naturally a nice person and speak gently unconsciously. On the other side, you will become angry and behave rudely in a place you simply do not want to go. Therefore, mostly people look calm, cool, and friendly at mediation places such as mosques, churches, mandirs, yoga centres, and temples.

Thoughts in unconscious mind always dictate us and show us the way to behave. You know when you are going to hospital in an emergency; you will become a little anxious, worried and depressed. You may drive rashly or slowly due to your unconscious thoughts going on. Oppositely, if you are going to marry, you will be cheerful, excited, and romantic in your behavior and conduct. Your thoughts would also become more imaginative and innovative at that time.

Beliefs about the information perceived are the strongest part of us that guide us in each moment of life. When someone behaves nicely in front of his friends, he might have a belief that friends must be given priority over others in life or any other belief conveying the similar meanings. On the contrary, one can behave rudely with his wife based on the belief that one should act like a lion in front of his family.

The last background is future orientation or association in mind. We behave according to our expectations and priorities. When we meet someone we think could give us something in the form of money, respect, comfort, or anything-tangible or intangible; we behave good, wise, compose and even empathetic. Whereas with the person who we think could never be able to support us in any form or may harm us in one way or the other, we use other tactics by behaving indifferent, rude, uninterested or even apathetic.

Thus, we change not only our attitude, rather behavior and thoughts according to our needs ahead at any particular time. We unconsciously get information from our backgrounds about the place we are acting in, people we are interacting with, a scenario in which we are dealing with others and about the benefits linked with those experiences. We calculate it all in the shortest possible period and then act. Usually we make mistakes and other people around us take it other way round, as they are not aware of our background knowledge of the event. Such mistakes or misperceptions may cost a high price if not understood properly in time. Therefore, one must try to fill the communication gap until his level best and should not leave a room for misperceptions or misunderstandings. Otherwise, things could become too complicated to solve!

Due to some misperceptions we encounter many types of conflicts in our daily life that normally drag us towards the unlimited depth of depression, anxiety and hopelessness. Though there are many cognitive therapies that try to change our brain's configuration or our ways of thinking, yet the process demands a lot of hard work and strong motivation towards a change at both ends. In short, it is not an easy way and most of us leave it in between.

Here, a very important phenomenon is missing and that is our perceptual understanding of the problem and its bondage/relationship with our immediate environment. Perceptions alone (without finding out their connections with immediate environment) cannot be altered/changed even through a hard wire of reasoning. Let's take an example. A child is very lazy, never interested in study, always makes some excuses, plays games instead, even though there is a good teacher available with good environment, good stuff and good techniques. The moment second child comes into the competition, the first one suddenly changes his attitude/behavior and acts as if he is no more a previous one. Now he is all together changed in a second. There could be several examples to quote in which we see the same person behaving differently due to a sudden change in his/her immediate environment.

Therefore, by having a real change in our environment, we can think of a perceptual change in our brain and a real change in our life. Our personalities are a mixture of the multitude of emotions and concepts and we choose some of them that suit our present needs and environment. We would say something now and the very opposite instead if there is any change in our environment. Have you noticed people talking to you on cell suddenly changing their tone when someone enters or leaves the room. Thus, we can say that our opinions, attitudes and behaviors are always subject to change due to our physical or perceptual environment.

You know things are perceived very differently through changing their recipes, color, conditions, or even packing. People face huge losses on items that carry unappealing or irrelevant color. Human beings are more sensitive to such changes. Our genes are our basic formulas. Our color of skin and shape of body parts, play a critical role in our self understanding and self perception. Similarly diverse psychological aspects, in our basic perceptual environment, play a critical role in understanding not only our self perception rather self misperception. Both physical and psychological health factors may drag us towards extremes of happiness or depression. Sometimes a little change in the related perceptual field brings the desired effects, and other times it will not work in years because we were heading in the wrong direction and/or at the wrong time.

There could be several other ways to change the environment. By changing place, by choosing an activity, by doing something else, by changing identity, by changing friends, by having something new, by removing something old etc. Changing your ways of eating, changing your ways of dressing or even talking could change your attitude in life. Sometimes buying flowers helps you in getting freshness and concentration; a little walk is all you need to get started; a refreshing, soothing bath is enough to feel energized and alive; and sometimes a compliment from a friend helps you to tune up. A little change is enough if it is going to execute some results otherwise, any big change like changing a country of residence, changing profession, even changing spouse would not work to eliminate your problems.

MISPERCEPTIONS WITH 'MORALITY'

When I search for humanity in literature, it usually comes with broad perspectives about the products like truth, honesty, empathy, selflessness, sincerity, and all other things related to these. Although these are not wrong perceptions about humanity, but we need a clear and concise concept about each of it in this complex era. For example, for truth, it must be clear what to say in a particular circumstance, whom to say truth, how to deliver it, when to deliver it and other related precise details. Sometimes, one single truth may take a person's life and alternatively that truth may also save someone's life. The same is true with other phenomena. We are for many times not sure about the reality of our morality or we are not trained in that sense that is why we miss many expressions of it.

We simply apply the morality, what we think morality is. In some cultures, respect is something related to standing up in front of others (like in Pakistan) while in others respect is something related to doing what is required (like in China). Similarly, in some cultures, asking for help is not respectable (in some parts of India) while in others it is the most convenient way to live (in UK). Nevertheless, in some places, one should take care of others' likes and dislikes with the exchange of highly valuable gifts (like in Pakistan) while in others one must give someone (as a gift) what he /she likes for him/her self (sender) plus it could be anything from a feather to a house (like Arab countries). There are a thousand examples to quote in this regard that prove that we address morality according to our own cultural, religious and personal needs.

Similarly, there are certain things in one culture that are thought as normal while in others are simply rude. For example, in one culture guests may be refused politely if you are busy (like in the UK), while in another one, guests simply cannot be refused or we will become rude. Like in Pakistan and India, guest cannot be refused at any time, for any cause. It is not polite to refuse them. Likewise, in some cultures, one must not enter others personal space while in others this is being proud, antisocial, and unfriendly. When we compare the rights and duties of women and men in different cultures of the world, we will find huge differences of different kinds. In short, whatever is your culture, you will feel that way and judge others accordingly.

When we define our morality according to our needs, we must respect others moral values as they are too according to their needs. However, there is a very delicate line between what is a cultural thing and a criminal thing. For example, in one culture, marriages are more about businesses whereas in others a marriage is a sacred entity and is more about religion. In some cultures, women are not treated equally like men and they need to know more about morality than men. In such cultures, girls have no right to ask about their status or should not expect the same status like boys. Their moral values vary for each section of the society and morality means total slavery of the poor class to the rich class/bosses/owners. From these examples, one must think what kind of cultures are these? Are they carrying up some values or criminal acts in the name of cultural beauties?

Thus, to take care of someone's culture when you know it is not worth taking care, is more about harming him/her than benefiting. Whenever we encounter something dangerous, alarming, negative, in the name of morality, we must not obey, irrespective of its origin or root cause. We must obey the moral rules that are in the interest of humanity overall. If there is any rule that is neither harming anyone nor benefiting, then it is up to us to follow it or not to follow. We, being the best judge, can set a moral guideline for us and others that proves best or we can choose to adapt (already set world criteria of being human) otherwise.

MISPERCEPTIONS WITH 'NEGATIVITY"

Negativity and its side effects are very common among positive psychologists. What about negativity and its positive effects! Are we wrongly blessed with negativity or there is some special cause for it. There are as many answers to this question as many people in this world. What I am going to highlight is that negativity is not useless rather more powerful and influential than positivity. The real positive people confront with their negativity first and then become positive. They cannot get rid of negative emotions by choice; they have to learn about how to deal with negative feelings and negative circumstances in the best possible way.

Negative sphere of mind is not something to ignore. It is not positivity rather negativity that causes all troubles and sufferings. All of us know about so-called golden rules of positivity, even then we are dealing with unsolved, complicated and constant mental anxieties of different kinds. We just cannot get rid of our web of needs, complaints, and sufferings (of past, present or future) so easily. It is not a fool's paradise that the moment we wish to live in the moment and start living!

From the word 'negativity', I mean things we do not like, things we think are not good for us, people we do not like, people we think are not our friends, and all other events that we think are against our wish, are negative indeed. We usually suffer from our negativity and while leaving it aside, ignoring it bluntly, work on positivity. Although it is important to follow your interests, but it is more important to check your dislikes. If you know your limitations and you try to deal with them positively, you will be much more positive and less negative as a result.

Well, we all know what beliefs are negative and what are positive in a broad sense, but for the trivia more specific and personal matters, we are confused between positivity and negativity. Sometimes we take a thing as negative, but it proves to be positive. Sometimes we think someone is positive and he/she proves to be negative or negative for us. Therefore negativity being an important human trait that influences all our lives badly and severely, must be explored more in detail as we are for most of the time in trouble due to negativity, not positivity.

Moreover, it is important to know that in negativity, not all negative thoughts are negative in nature; some are cruel/bitter realities/ truths of life that need a real attention from us. Not all negative memories need to eliminate rather some of them need to keep with us to get some lessons from and to become cautious for the sake of our safety. To elaborate the concept, for example, a killer needs not to feel better after killing someone, he must feel guilt/sorry to become normal after sometime. An abused one needs not to forgive his/her abuser in a second; he/she might get hurt again in the future by such attitude if he/she does not bother or take any necessary steps to eliminate the abuses.

Positive psychologists think we receive peace and happiness when we send gratitude in the universe. True, but sometimes, we are too kind and people get benefit from it, and finally put us in trouble in one way or the other. If you have a past with full of miserable relationship memories, you would always be advised to forget or forgive! It is not a button that will be turned off suddenly. Although we know it is better to forgive, but it needs to make clear how to forgive, how many times to forgive to the same person, after forgiving how to maintain the relationship etc. If you are blindly forgiving others, especially evil groups of society;

In the same context, it is important to keep friends, but it is more important to understand your enemies. If you try to deal with your enemies wisely and humanly, it will improve your positivity and reduce your negativity as well. Similarly, if you want to hold beliefs that give you strength, it will be better to work on your negative beliefs first. If you analyze truly, many of your negative beliefs will prove negative and you will improve your positivity instead.

Let us consider some more examples: suppose you are equipped with fearful feelings – a kind of negative emotion. These feelings always help you when your enemy is around. Imagine you are full of jealousy-another kind of negative emotion. Such emotions again boost your love for your beloved when he/she will come to know about it. Likewise, when you feel low self-esteem, you strive hard to feel better and thus struggle for a higher level of self-esteem. When you feel depressed, you go to the nature to rest in peace and harmony. Plus, when you feel dejected or humiliated, you come to know the value of truth and humanity.

Life goes on and you learn from negative people a lot. You come to know the worth of being human, the value of care, kindness and love, the meanings of honesty and sincerity, and ultimate solution to wandering mind and soul. Your comparison gives you more horizons to distinguish between good and bad and you are no more an innocent being to just absorb the day light and cry in the darkness.

Sometimes we need negative emotions to save lives. For example, a person who could not face injustice, might be utilizing his/her angry emotions for a good cause. Taking another example, a person could not tolerate lazy attitude in his/her personality. Here again the negative emotions of intolerance are giving him/her a tendency to increase control. The same is true for the people who are over suspicious about others. This negative trait sometimes saves them from being cheated, molested or treated unfairly. So people, who know what negativity is in a real sense, prove to be very positive. They know how to use their negativity in the most positive way and thus become positive.

Negativity is the exam for the positive ones. One must prove his/her self to be a positive one even in hard times or under negative circumstances. One must understand that this negativity is going to make him/her stronger and more powerful. This negativity will prove how much positive the person is!

There is a big difference between our negative and positive emotions and our negative and positive traits. Our emotions have two sides and each of it is there to protect our survival and existence fully. Whereas our negative personality traits exist to condemn, to stop, to control, and to eliminate with effort. We are not born with our negative traits, but with our negative emotions. Our emotions must not become part of our negative traits. Till the time our emotions (negative or positive) are going to save us and prove a source of energy for our happiness and survival, we are blessed. When we feel we are overwhelmed with our negative emotions and they are delimiting our positivity, we are becoming negative day by day. As we are not getting for what we are blessed with – negativity.

In short the negative emotions are there to deal with negative people, negative circumstances, and to understand our own negativity. When we learn the real meanings of negativity, we use our negativity against negativity- we become positive resultantly.

WRONG GENERALIZATIONS- ANOTHER KIND OF MISPERCEPTION:

Generalization is a process, a key to success and a tool to deal with care in most of the research work. The best of the researches, nowadays, base their findings on the validity of generalizations and limitations. Not a single research work would ever be able to generalize its results to the whole of the world. So the process of generalization of results to other (unrelated and out of the scope) parts of the world/subjects will provide us with the most uncommon and crucial findings- wrong generalizations.

For example, a research work conducted to study Asian women's psychology and especially of below average and unemployed group. In this research, only this category (below average and unemployed) would benefit from the findings not the other Asian women. If someone thinks the results are applicable to other categories as well, then he/she must prove it through other research work. People who see the results, in general, are not aware of such limitations as well as delimitations of the research work or ignore them unconsciously.

Given the above discussion is not for doing any research work rather to understand our human mind. We tend to generalize the findings in our brain as early as possible. Whenever we meet someone new in our life, we tend to perceive him/her at once and evaluate our experience later on. Suppose we say, " the man in black suit, looking tall and handsome, is caring and smart too". The next time we see someone like him (tall and in black suit, for example), we generalize our new experience based on our old experience and say, "he seems to be caring by his looks, gestures and personality overall".

Taking another example, you see someone from Pakistan and have a bad experience with him by chance. The next time you see any Pakistani, you will say, 'he seems to be a dishonest and swindler by his looks and personality'. You will remember your bad experience unconsciously or consciously and generalize the result to other Pakistanis. You will not realize that your one bad experience with only one man cannot be justified to other persons as they are from the same country, but from different categories (might have different status in education, social life, family structure, job, and many other fields).

Children make the generalizations too. Their generalizations are not very strong in the beginning, but if they are not mediated in time, they may become a part of their thoughts/beliefs in adulthood. Say, your child picks a black chocolate to eat and she feels the taste is not so good. The next time you will notice that she is hesitant in picking up any black thing to eat with the fear of having bad taste. Similarly, there are many live examples where children generalize very quickly and parents /care givers need to educate them on time. Otherwise, their wrong generalizations would become a part of their personality traits forever.

Generalization is not only limited to bad examples/experiences rather to the positive and healthy ones too. Have you met someone nice from another country? Do you remember your first love? Have you ever worked with some good organization? Have you met any caring relative? Do you know any sales person personally? Do you personalize any brand? Do you love any specific animal? Ok. Now do you feel the same feeling in your heart whenever you meet someone from the same nation, someone looking like your first love, someone part of the same organization, the same named friend or relative, another salesman from the same company, another product of the same brand, and the alike animal you love? Yes, you do generalize your feelings unconsciously. So it will not be wrong to say that we tend to generalize our experiences based on merely vague and limited information. Not only this, we strongly recommend them to others irrespective of their true nature-positive or negative.

By contrast, we should be very careful in our dealings with others, especially to strangers as they too are going to generalize their feelings for us. They may say in the future, people with big eyes are cruel or people of this nation are gentle or people speaking such language, are humble, or people with round faces are nasty or anything like that. In this way, we set examples in others brains to generalize the results. If we are nice, caring, gentle, responsible, sharing and well mannered, others will not only perceive us rather perceive alike us in the same manner (generalize us). If we are rude, harsh, strict, impolite, stern, aggressive, and stubborn, others not only perceive us as we are rather will not give any good note to the same category we belong to in general. Therefore, each of us is a trend setter on behalf of our own general category.

It becomes more important when we travel and represent our specific category as a part of a big nation. It becomes more important when we meet someone who does not belong to our category in terms of religion, sex, profession, social quo and education wise. The same rule applies to the same category, but the impact is stronger to the other category persons than the same or similar people like us.

MISPERCEPTIONS IN COMMUNICATIONS:

Talking to people is very common to communicate our feelings. We are not so sure how much we are successful in this effort. Sometimes we talk about something and the other one drives another meaning instead. Actually he/she interprets according to his/her own coding system. The other one is more likely to use that piece of information to his/her interests and that might interfere with your ones. Therefore, it is highly recommended not to speak carelessly or speak a little if you want to ensure your security.

To perceive someone's whole personality, it is very important to fill in the blanks while considering all aspects of the personality. We can never access anything from a single talk or a couple of talks with someone about only one or two topics of interest. It will be like watching a small part of a movie that is never suffice for our information to conclude the moral of the story. Thus we need to consider many things before reaching a conclusion about our perception of the other person:

• While talking to others, we unconsciously care about other's personalities and try to speak accordingly and the same is true for the other person.

• The perception of a thing is dramatically changed when it threatens our security. Whenever our interests are challenged, we change our thinking and guard our safety first unconsciously.

• Our general characteristics such as being active, beautiful, happy, loving cool, hyper, and lazy rely mostly on our interpretation of these traits. Most importantly, it is a matter of area context and scenario. If we think we are an active person, it does not mean we are active in all areas of life rather in some specific areas or matters of life. Hence, to access meanings from one trait will be quite misleading unless we know it in detail with respect to its limitation.

• We need similar interests to talk to each other, to establish friendship, and maintain friendship in the long run. I am surprised to know that people get married, having no common area of interest.

• Some of us behave decently and love to express their humbleness in manners, but cannot express their true feelings in words. While others express their true feelings and behave differently. Some can express as well as behave accordingly. Many among us follow others blindly in terms of speaking, behaving and feeling. That is why we are becoming fool in the hand of marketers. We have no control over our desires and follow others. Most of the advertisers get the benefit of our ignorance of our needs and exploit us in the trickiest manner- we unconsciously adapt their thinking style.

• Words in claims carry different meanings for different people. Everyone explains the phenomenon in a different way. For example, for you 'love' means you are ready to spend some time with someone with true, honest and good feelings. Alternatively, your partner may think 'love' means being together always mentally, not physically. Therefore, one word carries different meanings (patterns of thoughts) for different people. Let's take another example in this regard. For a person 'a', 'care' means to help someone in need (physically) and for the person 'b', to help with money is the biggest help. Due to such diversity of thought, we sometimes argue with each other and do not find a common ground to settle down.

• One person cannot totally think from another's point of view. Rather, it is next to impossible to comprehend others true perceptions completely. At the same time, we cannot deny the fact that empathy is the key to all different kinds of relationship misperceptions.

• Words in combination with a tone mirroring our true feelings have a stronger impact on others when we talk about things. To feel pure and good while speaking is a thing to learn, not the instinct/god gifted talent. Anyone can work on it and can practice to achieve the desired results associated with it.

All communication is to solve our problems, to be closer to each other and to have a good social life as well. If you follow all communication rules, but the real message does not convey then it is of no use. Like it does not matter whether you sleep for six hours or eight hours, the real thing that matters is your real satisfaction or freshness that comes from deep sound sleep. Similarly, it does not matter you buy things or not, you go for swimming or not, you enjoy parties or not, you have lots of shopping or not, what matters is your pure satisfaction you derive out of your experiences. Thus, our communication must create an atmosphere of perceptual understanding among our listeners – should not promote misperception otherwise.

Thanks

CONCLUSION

There are as many misperceptions in the world as many perceptions. We in one way or the other become victim of some of misperceptions in our daily life. Our concepts prove our misperceptions right in our opinion. We always blame others for our misperceptions and suffer a lot. There could be several causes for our perceptual misunderstanding, but the result is the same: misperception.

Not all the perceptual knowledge is misperceived. Being a conscious human being, we understand our true feelings very well. But sometimes, in spite of our whole intellect and smartness, we are trapped. We are stuck. We are torn apart. We regret. Then we realize that we have misperceived someone, some thing, or some experience as a whole. It took us too long to get true meanings from our vague experiences.

In the light of the above discussion (in different parts of this book), we can easily conclude that some misperceptions are conceptual(misperceptions about morality and negativity), some are relationship oriented (misperceptions in communications), some are habitual(wrong generalizations), and many are due to background diversity.

I hope that the information about misperceptions given would prove useful in making you vigilant, cautious and alert before perceiving any information truly. I hope you will make friends with more confidence and will not commit judgment errors in perceiving people around you. I wish you could predict better about your misperceptions and do not waste your time and energy on non-profitable tasks, unattractive themes and unhealthy options of life ahead.

Your understanding of misperceptions would guide you throughout your life. However, you might explore more ways to explain the construct in the most convincing way. In one way or the other, we must work together to resolve the perceptual complexity fully to become a perfect, vigilant, and unique human being.

Thanks

About The Author:

Mona Aeysha Khalid, PhD, is an Educational and Developmental Psychologist, have been working as a Teacher, Counselor, and Researcher in several institutes of China, Pakistan and Cambodia.

Her major areas of interest are: self –esteem, self-concept, conceptual psychology, belief psychology, self psychology, preferential psychology, cultural psychology and women psychology.

You are always welcome to contact her via email:

mei3na4@gmail.com

Tweet @monaaeysha

Thanks
Dr Mona